LITTLE WHISPERS

Edited by

Sarah Andrew

First published in Great Britain in 2001 by
ANCHOR BOOKS
Remus House,
Coltsfoot Drive,
Peterborough, PE2 9JX
Telephone (01733) 898102

HB ISBN 1 85930 900 3
SB ISBN 1 85930 905 4

FOREWORD

Anchor Books is a small press, established in 1992, with the aim of promoting readable poetry to as wide an audience as possible.

We hope to establish an outlet for writers of poetry who may have struggled to see their work in print.

The poems presented here have been selected from many entries. Editing proved to be a difficult task and as the Editor, the final selection was mine.

I trust this selection will delight and please the authors and all those who enjoy reading poetry.

Sarah Andrew
Editor

CONTENTS

I HATE BOYS

I   hate boys, they make me sick
    Sometimes I just want to give them a kick

H umorous and clever they think they are
    But they're not, not by far
A cting as if they know everything
    I hate it when they try to sing
T rusting them is a big mistake
    If they seem sensible, it's all just fake
E ntertaining and amusing they try to be
    Ignoring them is the key

B oys, boys, they're all the same
    Make silly jokes that are lame
O h! I wish they would just grow up
    Talking non-stop of football and World Cup
Y et, sometimes they can be okay
    When they listen to us girls and obey
S till, there is always hope
    For the time being we have to learn to cope.

Tanjina Jalil (10)

MY BROTHER

Mark is a spider creeping up the wall,
dropping down to the floor and then going up the door.
Spinning, weaving, climbing, running, chuckling, thinking.

Mark is a pixie laughing, whispering, tricking, hiding in the tree,
making you jump higher than you've ever jumped before,
falling over with glee. Then joking, telling, getting away.

Mark is ivy growing up the tree, being as clever as can be,
making you trip and do a double flip, landing on your back in agony.
Then he will crawl away and say
'Hey Claire, I bet you can't find me in this tree, come on,
come and catch me, *he, he, he.*'

Claire Lovatt (10)

BOYS AND GIRLS

Boys can be bad,
Boys can be sad.
Boys can be strong,
Boys can be wrong.
Boys can be tall,
Boys can be small.
Boys can be cool,
Boys can rule.

Sarah Eden (11)

Girls can be neat,
Girls can be sweet.
Girls can be pretty,
Girls can be witty.
Girls can be cute,
Girls can be brute.
Girls can be cool,
Girls can rule.

A MAGICAL SUMMER

The wind has ceased and springtime is ending,
Up in the heavens, the weather is bending
Its work complete, off scuttles the rain,
And out comes the sun, shining and vain.

Over the hills and far away,
All the sprites come out to play
Kicking their legs and flicking their wings,
Dancing round the fairy rings.

Pixies are running out of the wood,
To claim their prizes for getting up to no good
The elves are preparing a field performance,
With singing and dancing, an event of importance.

The Queen of Spring gets ready to bow,
And place the crown on the Summer King's brow
While the gnomes and imps prepare the food
Beans and potatoes, uncooked and crude.

Then when all is done, the festivities over,
All head off for a night in the clover
All through the garden the band causes a tremor,
The perfect start to a magical summer.

Hollie Lewis (12)

THE GOBLIN POEM

When the goblins come
I kneel and pray
Listening carefully
To what they say.

Words of truth
They do sing
No gift compares
To what they bring.

With the goblins
The world does battle
You know their spell
When the pots rattle.

In their careful hands
My soul I bequeath
Forever in goblins
I do believe!

Mick Deamer

I SIT AT THE WINDOW . . .

I sit at the window;
As the water falls down.
Is it the rain running down the glass?
Or the tears dripping down my cheeks?
I look inside.
There's a fire warm and inviting,
Though I'd rather freeze to death,
Than give in to bribery now.
I see the train outside.
Leaving, back to London.
I feel its pull on me.
I won't let go, never.
I feel the clouds in the sky.
Swarming over me, engulfing me,
Blinding, choking, preventing me,
From seeing.
Are they clouds of the storm, the train?
Or are they clouds of the mind?
My heart is like a hand.
Reaching out to that of my past life.
We're at a junction, we try to grasp tight
But we fly apart and I fall down,
Bang! Dark, alone, frightened, scared.
The string digs into my shoulder,
And I take it and the box off and throw the mask down.
'To save us' well what if we don't want to be.
Isn't family more important than individual safety?
Love is all the safety we need.
The warmth from inside reaches me.
It tries to thaw my blood.
Is it the warmth of the fire?
Or that of my 'new' family?
Whichever I don't care.
I don't want to be here and I don't want
To change.

I don't want to be in the countryside.
I want to be in London with mother.
Tears run down my face.
The smoke from my mind clouds it.
I can't think straight.
The warmth of my 'new' family reach me.
All three begin to fight.
I try to escape.
I bury my head in my knees.
But as the fight is in my head,
It doesn't go away or help.
Oh leave me alone,
Go away.
Shadow growing and growing,
Forever behind me, waiting to pounce.
Like a bomb waiting to explode.

Jenny Campbell (14)

PET TALK

Pets are such a comfort,
they understand each word.
I know this may sound strange,
and also quite absurd.

I have a little budgie,
Sparkle is his name.
Although I've had him for three years,
he is not very tame.

He's jumpy when you move quite quick,
and with a sudden noise.
Especially when his cage gets knocked,
by little girls and boys.

His colours are mainly blue and black,
with white specks in between.
And if you can get close to him,
pale green feathers can be seen.

I'd like him to rest on my hand,
when I give him food and drink.
Instead he backs away from me,
and gives a cheeky wink.

He looks a very pretty boy,
as he moves about his cage.
And when he dances on his perch,
he should be on centre stage.

When I get back home,
after being out all day.
He looks at me with beady eyes,
and wants to say, please stay.

I know that Sparkle loves me,
because when I'm feeling down,
he chirps and tweets to let me know
that I am not alone.

We must look after all our pets,
whether big or small.
Inside or out of doors,
because the good Lord treasures all.

Teresa Street

WISH YOU WERE NOT HERE

Over across the Irish Sea,
Miles away from home.
There's a place
You might have heard of,
Called the Millennium Dome.
It's full of science and maths
And loads of boring stuff
To tell you the truth,
I'd rather sit home,
And pick from my ear . . . bits of fluff.

Donna O'Connor (10)

A NEW COUSIN

A new cousin
for the family tree
it's a strange coincidence
she was born on the same month as me
October's the month
our birthdays will be
she will be celebrating her first
but it's ten for me.

Grant Pillians (9)

THE BUTTERFLY

I found a little butterfly
Just lying on the floor,
It was missing one of its legs
And both its wings were torn.

I took that little butterfly
And put it in a jar,
It looked at me so gratefully
Its eyes twinkling like stars.

It only stayed a few short days
As I had really known,
But finding it that day, makes me want to say
Please just leave animals alone!

Katie Swales (10)

THE PERFECT GIFT

I don't need a trike.
I don't need a bike.
I don't need a cat.
Nor a baseball bat.

I don't need any of these
Because I have the perfect gift
And the perfect gift is Mum.

I don't need a brilliant book.
I don't need to learn how to cook.
I don't need a pretty face.
I don't need to win a race.

I don't need any of these
Because I have the perfect gift
And the perfect gift is Mum.

Ashley Davies (10)

REMEMBERING BACK!

Remembering back in 1991,
Was something that I would never forget.
When jokes were told, which I would never quite get,
Remembering when I was 1 . . . !

My first steps were incredible,
Well, that's what my mum would say.
I was *brill!* Day after day after day.
My legs are incredible.

My first word was very impressive,
I would say 'Mama' when I wanted something.
And 'Mama' when I was scribbling,
That was my very first word.

But sometimes I still remember back in 1991,
When jokes were told which I would never get.

Beth Grason (9)

CHANGE

As we walk down the street things are changing at our feet
People don't stop and stare to see what things we have to share
Flowers wilt and birds will die but no one cares
As technology creeps in our mind we leave the natural world behind
As we walk down the street things are changing at our feet.

Abigail Johnston (12)

WINTER

Decking of silence, night's cold breeze,
sitting by the fire because I don't want to freeze.

Sitting by the fire which is very hot,
eating soup from a small grey pot.

My little black cat stretching on the fluffy mat,
nothing bad comes between her and her Christmas rat.

Olivia Lewis (9)

STUPID GIRLS!

I hate stupid girls
They make me want to hurl
They're never in with trends
It makes my hair stand on their ends
They are so thick
They'll never get a click
I'm glad I am a boy
Some girls are nice
They're not ugly like mice
Some are like a spice.

Michael Swan (11)

GIRLS

Girls are iky, picky and disgusting.
But adults think they're nice as spice
And worth twice as much as me.

But when they get a crush on you
You have to beg them to set you free.

Their clutches are treacherous, they can nip
Clip and tear and their screams make my hair stand on end.

Never enter their lair,
If you do, do it with great care
Enter if you dare!

Jason Murray (12)

WHAT GIRLS THINK ABOUT BOYS

There are boys in my class, there are boys in my house
Wherever I go there are boys around.

They roll on the ground and don't care a bit.
They talk about football and shout at the TV.

They think they are fit and better than girls
But us girls don't sit around and watch TV.

Their rooms are a mess
And they couldn't care less.

I hate it when boys hit girls with the balls
And say 'Oh sorry, it wasn't my fault.'

Boys are so annoying,
I wish they didn't exist.

Debbie Smith (12)

GIRLS ON BOYS

Boys are like stars that twinkle in the sky,
Sometimes they're good, and sometimes they are bad.

The boring thing about boys is they don't like shopping,
But it's different when we have to watch them playing football.

Girls and boys like the same sort of things,
So I don't see the point when girls and boys argue.

Especially when it's about something I know they both like.
So the point I'm trying to make is boys and girls are equal!

Fiona Mack (11)

GIRLS

Nudge, nudge, nudge goes my elbow,
as the girl next to me shoves it.
Chat, chat, chat as she asks me stuff,
and gets me into trouble for talking.
But mostly she talks to her friends,
it drives me absolutely bananas.
That's just what I know,
can't say what I don't.

Colin Tipton (11)

BOYS!

Boys always fight and always feel they are right.
They like to think they are the best
A lot better than the rest
They like to copy the TV stars
Like Ali G and David Beckham
Where as girls would love to be Posh Spice
Because she looks very nice.

Boys are immature and silly
Always thinking they have the latest gear
But all they need is a 'box' on their ear
I am glad I am a girl
Because boys are really bad
And drive me very mad!

Sarah Gosman (11)

BOYS!

Nudge, nudge at my elbow,
Hey, hey, do you know about so and so?

Go away, leave me alone
They act as though they are only one!

But some boys can be really nice,
So quiet, just like mice!

I get my work finished,
The teacher is pleased.

I get a star on the chart, what a start!

Susan Gosman (11)

GIRLS!

Their harmful nip, pinch and tear,
Is something that I can't bear.
Screeching and screaming,
Their eyes are always beaming.
I wouldn't dare,
Go near them when they have an angry red flare.
They think that we are thick,
Because we always fall for their silly tricks.

There are some that are nice,
And as harmful as mice.
There are some that are smart,
And could make a motored kart.
There are some that are tall,
You can get girls bossy, bubbly, ugly or nice,
But boys will always be better and more nice.

Andrew Munro (11)

MY VIEW OF BOYS

Boys have got football in their veins
It's always in their brain
It drives me insane

Boys try to act cool
But they're really fools
Especially at school

Boys never grow
So what have they got to show
When they're ninety-four

Most boys are naughty
Some are nice
But they're not all sugar 'n' spice.

Nicola Melrose (11)

GIRLS ON BOYS

Boys like football
I don't know how
Boys can't understand
Why teachers ask them to behave

Boys don't listen
They forever have something to talk about
Boys are daydreamers
They forever find something to think about

Boys are boring
They always talk about football
Boys are weird
They are in a world of their own

Boys are totally different from girls.

Mandy MacEwan (11)

POSH GIRLS

Boy I hate posh girls
they never, ever care about other people
perfect, fussy, posh girls.
Never trust them to do anything right
because if you do they'll lie,
and run away without doing what you told them to do.
Why?
I'll tell you why,
because they never have time for us boys.

So never, ever, ever, ever trust a big, bossy,
selfish, fussy, perfect and rich posh girl.
One more thing, don't ever ask them out
because it will be the biggest mistake you ever make.

Scott Macdonald (10)

Boys

Boys watch too much telly,
Their brains are like jelly.
Boys are big and fat like my cat,
She is called Pat.
Boys are freaks because they have no cheeks,
Boys can't spell because they can't say Adele.
Boys are lazy because they hate daisies,
Boys are idiots.
They pick their nose with their toes,
They are just *freaks.*

Sophie Lee (9)

BOYS ABOUT GIRLS

Girls are horrible, their rooms always smell,
Every time you go in their room
They'll be lying snoring on their bed,
Then when you go out to play,
Then come back to play in your room,
They'll be playing your computer
When you tell them to go out your room,
They go away crying to your mum,
Then you get a row from your mum
Then we probably get grounded for two months.

John Jackson (10)

GIRLS ABOUT BOYS

Boys are smelly, heads filled with jelly.
Watch too much telly.
Bedroom's a pit, always playing football.
Boys are thick, they eat until they are sick.
They try to hit but miss.
Boys are rotten, made of cotton.
That's what little boys are made of.
Think they're cool but in their sleep they drool.
Boys are cruel.
I think girls rule.

Nikki Tipton (9)

BOYS ABOUT GIRLS

Girls, girls paint their nails and toes,
Girls, girls are so smelly that their brains are full of jelly,
Girls, girls are so silly and they all fancy Billy,
Girls, girls are weak in all the days of the week,
Girls, girls are so spoilt because they cry all the time,
Girls are scared of the dark,
Girls, girls.

Mutassim Ghazali (9)

BOYS

Boys are smelly, ugly and lazy.
They come from outer space.
You never get a good answer from them.
They're a waste of space.
Girls are better than boys.
They think they rule the world.
But the most annoying thing about boys
Out of: lazy, ugly and smelly, is
Lazy!

Lyn Crook

BOYS ABOUT GIRLS

Girls are always putting on make-up and it's disgusting.
Girls run slow, they're dirty and lazy and they have no brains.
They're messy, bossy and disobedient, they are smelly, revolting girls.
Girls are rubbish at football, they don't have tidy bedrooms.
They are thick and soft.
They have skinny heads, they think they're tough but they're not.

Keir Johnston (10)

Boys!

There is this boy I don't like
His name is Spike!
He eats slugs and bugs
He sits beside my friend
She says 'Oh when will it end?'
I am only joking, he doesn't eat slugs and bugs
But it seems like it
In the playground he can hardly run
Because he is so fat
I go running right past him!
He asks people out every day of the week
Especially my best friend

B   oys are so annoying!
O   h, I don't exactly hate them but I don't like them!
Y   eah! They shout when our team wins. They really hurt my ears.
S   hut up, they would say to you.

Kirsty Mackenzie (10)

GIRLS ABOUT BOYS

Boys are smelly and rude
Their bedrooms are messy, clothes everywhere
Toys everywhere as well
Boys would eat anything even if it was mouldy
And had been lying there for three weeks.
They think they are tough, but they lie about all day and watch TV.
Boys think they are the best, come on, they can't be right,
Girls are the best.

Joanne Whigham (10)

BOYS

The opposite sex are definitely boys,
Their names are different, for example, Roy.
They can be sick or sad or cool,
But most play up when we're at school.

Boys sing and dance and laugh and play,
But most annoy me every day.
Some I like and some I hate,
Some I know I'll never date.

Most girls say boys are sad,
If all were they'd drive me mad,
But as they're not I am relieved,
For I will never be deceived.

I have lots of friends that are all boys,
I've played with some since baby toys.
They can be horrid or quite nice,
With one I have shared head lice.

My favourite boys are wild and mad,
With them I have been very bad.
Forever more I rest my case,
Boys are part of the human race.

So here I come to a conclusion,
Boys are nothing but an illusion.
Everyone is equal (I say),
So without them we wouldn't last another day.

Carmen García-Lillis (11)

BOYS WILL BE BOYS!

Boys are so immature, noisy and they have the most yucky smell,
And they drive you up the wall like hell!
When it's assembly in the hall,
They just sit and talk about football!

Boys are gooly, creepy and go bump in the night,
But some are sensitive and nice, yeah right!
They muddy things up which aren't even their own,
They can't even be bothered to cut their hair so it's all overgrown!

Boys act all cool with their mates,
But most of them can't even get through the garden gate!

We'll never change the fact that *boys will be boys*,
So they might as well stay at home with their *toys!*

Katie Senior (11)

BOYS

Boys are big,
Boys are sad,
They think they're good,
When they're bad.

Boys could be cool,
Boys could be good,
They like to roll,
Around in mud.

Some boys are nice,
Some boys are silly,
They are usually late,
As they dally and dilly.

Lindsey Cheetham (11)

BOYS

Boys are sad
Boys are mad
They are weird
When they're bad.

Boys would be cool
If they were good
But when they're not
They never could.

If you want to
See up close
A boy who makes
The world so gross.

Just look around
The corner now
And you will see one
Just see how!

Eva Flint (12)

BOYS

Boys are disgusting!
I think they are revolting!
They pick their noses,
And stamp on roses!
They pull your hair,
It is just not fair!

Some act nice,
But they really are spice.
They don't really care
About destroying your teddy bear
(That's the bad side).

Good side:
Boys can help with work,
Boys can play,
But, I am sorry,
That is possibly
The only good thing to say.

Boys are smart,
But their behaviour is bad,
Which makes the teacher sad.

That is my report of boys,
Now please let me play with toys.

Elisa de Souza

BOYS

Boys are boys, there's no doubt about that,
Some tall, some smelly, some thin, some fat,
Boys are rude
And most are crude
And I'm relieved to say, I won't see them every day,
Boys can be nice, boys can be pants
But then again some can dance!
Most of what I've said today
Can mainly go both ways
I've come to my conclusion, my end
I hope I do not offend.

Ellen Powell (11)

A POEM ABOUT BOYS

Boys can be kind,
Boys can be nice,
But not like girls
Who are sugar and spice

Boys play up,
Boys like to fight,
Boys like to show off
With all their might.

Boys can be brothers,
Boys can be friends,
But most of the time
They drive you round the bend.

Boys on the other hand,
Can be loving and giving,
Boys can be true friends
So I thank them for living.

Holly Darby (9)

GIRLS ON BOYS

Girls are quiet, boys are loud
Girls can barely whisper but boys can really shout
Boys only think about three things -
Football, PlayStations and Pokémon,
Girls can sit down for ages,
Boys can't sit down for two minutes and they're always out,
Girls may be loud, but not as loud as boys, never, no way
Not in a million years!

Adeesha Iyaloo (10)

MY THOUGHTS ON GIRLS

Girls are fat
Girls are thin
Girls don't go near rubbish bins
Girls are tall
Girls are small
Girls have high heels and sometimes fall
Girls smell bad
Girls smell nice
Some smell like sugar and some like spice
Girls have hair, girls are bald
Girls have secrets, never told
Girls are naughty, girls are good
I could like them, I really could . . .

Liam Rusk (9)

GIRLS

Their giggling is annoying and so is their kicking.
Whenever they get the chance they chat for hours and hours.
Their rowdy screams fill the playground with fun and excitement.
But to me some girls are violent and enthusiastic.
Both boys and girls are as bad as each other.

David Murphy (10)

BOYS ON GIRLS

Girls, girls, they're all right
sometimes they're friends
sometimes they fight

Girls, girls, they like cuddly toys
and I think they might
actually like boys!

Girls, girls are good fun
when they chase after you
you have to run!

Girls, girls, cheer you up when you are down
that's nice of them,
they clear up all your frowns!

Girls, girls, are my friends
that's that
now the poem ends!

William English (11)

GIRLS

Girls are good fun to have around
But some drive you around the bend
Most are okay, but some are not
But they end up as good friends
Most of their lives they end up chatting and
Laughing, laughing and chatting
In all the time in this world they spend
Giggling and gossiping, gossiping and giggling
I think of them as civilised human beings
Who make life worth living in this
Small world of ours.

Dil Patel (10)

SOME GIRLS

Some girls are kind
Some girls don't mind
Some girls are pretty
Some girls are witty
Some girls are funny
Some girls have money
Some girls are mad
Some girls are bad
Some girls like boys
Some girls like toys
Some girls moan
Some girls groan
Some girls have power
Some girls like a flower
Some girls are weak
Some girls are unique
Some girls have dolls
Some girls have trolls
Some girls are nice
Some girls hate mice
Some girls read books
Some girls have looks.
Some girls, who needs them?

William Lines (10)

GIRLS!

Girls, girls are fussy and they scream.
Girls, girls are always on diets and don't eat ice-cream.
Girls, girls are silly and like wearing pink.
When I was young I thought -
'Girls, they stink.'

But now I'm 11
I've changed my mind
I know some girls who are kind.
They look fit, neat and cool.
My favourite girl doesn't go to my school.

James Bannister (11)

GIRLS

Girls are stupid,
Girls are fat,
They're just like a
Smelly old cat.
They like rag dolls,
And stupid toys,
And try to kid us
Harmless boys.
Girls are ugly,
Girls are thick,
They just make me
Sick, sick, sick.

This is my last verse,
It's got to be good,
I can say millions of horrible things
About girls, I could, I could, I could.
Girls are un-neat,
And don't like football,
They need to look at boys
If it means being cool.
Girls think they're the part,
And they know it all,
But if you think about it
Only some are fools.

Tyler Blake (10)

GIRLS

Girls, girls are good for your heart
The more you eat the more you . . . !
Girls are good, girls are sweet
Girls are good enough to eat.
Long blonde hair, big blue eyes
They are the ones that say the goodbyes.
Girls like boys, boys like girls
Especially the ones with curls.
Red hair, brown hair, short or long,
With the boys that's where they belong.
Fat or thin, thin or fat
I could take them to my flat.
Sugar, sugar, on the wall
Girls are the sweetest of them all.
One, two, three, four
They are the ones that we adore.
Five, six, seven, eight
They leave me standing at their gate.
Football is our way of life,
But girls just scream at Westlife.
Horses, dolls, clothes and hair,
For any of that we just don't care.
Girl power is all the rage,
That will change when I come of age.
Boys they spend their time fishing,
Girls spend theirs forever wishing.
Rollerblades they go missing,
When the girls come round and we start kissing.
Girls are great, girls are fun,
They really are the number one.

Anthony Papworth (9)

Boys

Some boys are fat, some boys are thin,
Some are clever but most are dim.
Some boys are small and some boys are tall,
Some boys are loud, some boys are quiet and
Some boys are just a riot.

Some boys are nice, some boys are nasty,
Some are just really ghastly.
Some boys think they're cool,
Some boys act the fool.

Some boys are clean,
Some boys are dirty and
Some smell like they're
A hundred and thirty.

Dianne Perry (11)

BOYS!

Boys never dress up smartly,
They never brush their hair.
I think they would rather stay in bed,
Because they don't really care.

Boys always stay up late,
Playing video games.
There is one boy who's really annoying,
His first name is James.

I really hate boys,
Apart from my dad.
All boys are silly,
And don't forget they're mad.

Rhona Lavis (9)

BOYS

Boys are mad
And drive me up the wall
They make me sad
But they play football

Off Jupiter they come
Or the sun probably
They are very dumb
Brains of boys are cobbly.

Little boys
Are very different by miles
Even though they make noise
And their toys are stacked up in piles.

Kirsty Griffin (10)

BOYS

Boys are a pain in the neck,
They play such stupid games,
Like falling off the deck,
Because their enemy's just killed them.

Every once in a while
They can be really funny.
But sometimes it's what they do,
Like if they trip over some books in a pile.

Boys are mostly brats,
They're always making trouble,
Boys are so much like rats,
They're dirty and over-running.

Boys are trouble makers,
They're always being told off.
Boys can never sit still,
Not even for a minute.

Boys each have a different personality,
They're all so different at heart,
I suppose not all boys like all girls like me,
The same as I don't like all boys.

Elizabeth Collins (10)

BOY POEM

Boys can be boisterous
  Boys can be mean
Boys can tease you
  Boys can make you scream
Boys think they're tough
  Boys can be rough
Boys can be kind
  Then we don't mind
Playing their games.

Jessica Ann Collingwood (10)

I DON'T LIKE BOYS VERY MUCH

I don't like boys very much
They always seem to smell so much
With dirty nails
Pockets full of snails
I don't like boys very much

I don't like my brother very much
He always argues with me so much
He's naughty and shouts
I give him lots of clouts
I don't like my brother very much

I don't like my uncle very much
He's always telling me off so much
He's big and fat
I call him a rat
I don't like my uncle very much.

Taidi Dibble (10)

BOYS

Boys can be very rough
That's why they think they're tough,
They all gather in a den
And try to be Action Men.

Creating mischief is their game
And looking for someone else to blame,
They can sometimes be quite good
But only when they think they should.

I think I like girls the best
Because boys are a bit of a pest,
Still they really aren't too bad
Because a boy grew up to be my dad.

Danielle Amber Currie (10)

BOYS

I hate boys, they are a pain,
and their work is just so lame,
let's just put it this way,
they do not have brains.

I have never met a single one
that is sensible.

All they do is sit around playing
on their Gameboys and picking noses
and spraying hoses at girls.

Oh yes and don't forget their hair gel
every day they come to school
with thick layers of hair gel on.

How I just hate boys.

Lillian Griffin (9)

ALL ABOUT BOYS

Boys are always fiddling,
fiddling with their hair.
They run around all day
playing football in the playground.
They love to hang around
waiting for a girl to see
if they will come
or even if they fail.
Because boys are always fiddling,
fiddling with their hair.

Lian Ford (10)

ISAAC

He is my brother
and I don't have another
He ran so far
That we had to pick him up in the car
He is so tall
And he is good at football
He is a bit of a pain
But I love him all the same.

Zelie Gibbs (7)

GIRLS

Girls giggling and running around
With pony tails swinging up and down
Hair blowing in the breeze
As they skip about -
Their chattering voices making a tune
While they are playing noisy games
Pretty girls with long eyelashes
And smooth skin
With gentle feelings in their hands
And sensitive thoughts in their heads.

Ross D'Arcy (7)

BOYS ON GIRLS

Girls like busy bees
Working in the class.
Then they play with dollies
As if they're grown-up mums.

I like all their kindness
They have for other kids.
But I can't stand all their bossiness
When they make up silly fibs.

So always bear this in mind
That your girlfriend could be
A pretty, cheeky mastermind.

But who cares?
Girls can play with boys
And boys can play with girls
Because we're so alike.

Benik Reef (8)

GIRLS ON BOYS

Boys like football,
Boys like dogs,
Boys like wearing smelly socks,
Boys, boys, boys,
Boys like Gameboys,
Boys like PlayStations,
Boys like Pokémon,
Boys, boys, boys,
Boys like James Bond,
Boys like The Simpsons,
Boys like Craig David,
Boys, boys, boys.

Olivia Lindsey (7)

UNTITLED

They look like Barbie girls, pretty make-up girls
They look nice and sweet
They play around, playing Barbie
Some don't, some play
Something else
They have horrible manners
At the table,
I don't like them
When they tease boys.
They are a pain in the neck
I like it when they play with me
They don't bully me
They are having such fun.

Connor Griffin (7)

BOYS 'N' GIRLS

There are these boys in my class
Which I'd rather not speak about and rather pass,
But as it's you I'll give you a clue.

They're dirty and smelly,
And they walk around with a very big belly,
'Cause they just sit in front of the telly.

They sit in class picking their noses,
You just want to get out the hoses.

They try to impress you by acting the clown,
But when they do it just gets you down,
And makes you put on a massive frown.

These are not the goriest details of all.

One boy has pet mice,
Which is not very nice,
And has given everybody *lice!*

Kaiya Richards (12)

BOYS

They think they're hot,
When really, they're not.

They think they're cool,
If they're naughty at school.

They think they can fight,
Yeah right!

They think they're so tough,
Oh, I've had enough!

Carla Ewer (11)

BOYS ARE ...

Boys are stinky potato peelings,
Rotten snails
Disgusting slug trails
Dark sludgy green
Yesterday's leftovers with cream.

Zara Turvey (9)

GIRLS ARE . . .

Girls are stinky smelly turnips
Cooked orange carrots
Flying buzzing insects
Disgusting purplish pink.

Jordan Turvey (7)

BOYS

I don't want to sound at all mean
But boys never seem to be clean.
They can sometimes act really thick
And make you feel incredibly sick.

Boys have got a really deep voice
And always make lots of noise.
They behave like great big babies
And go mad when they see pretty ladies.

When a boy finally gets a date
He would probably turn up late.
Then they start to have a wash,
Clean their teeth and act all posh.

Boys are always really vain
And just like babies, they're a pain.
They look in the mirror and comb their hair
And what happens around them, they don't care.

Boys work in very strange ways
And get worse through passing days.
It seems that boys don't impress girls at all
Whether fat or thin or short or tall.

After all of this that I've said
There is a name that pops in my head
It turns out there is another
And that boy is my brother.

He's not the same as all the rest
As nice, he would pass the test
Not all boys are quite that bad
And of that, I'm very glad.

Donna Austin (11)

BOYS

Boys can be very good,
but not when they play in the mud.

Boys can be good at art,
Maybe because they eat jam tarts.

Boys can be good at maths,
When they're older they might make rafts.

Boys can act silly at a party
Perhaps they think they're doing karate.

Boys can be very mad,
They remind me of my dad!

Laura Sleath (7)

BOYS

Boys are noisier, rougher and pretend to be tougher than girls,
most boys have spiky hair when we girls prefer curls.
They like mud and not make-up on their face
and they clap their hands before saying grace.
But are they really that different to us?
When they are badly hurt they still also make a fuss.

They call us silly for playing with dolls,
but Action Men are only dolls that can do forward rolls.
And just like girls, their best time of day
Is when it's time to go out and play.

Lydia Clarke (8)

BAD BOYS AND GOOD GIRLS

There are bad little boys, we are good little girls
That's because the teachers say this

Bad boys have bad table manners
Good girls have good table manners

Bad boys have their shirts hanging out
Good girls have their shirts tucked in

Bad boys throw stuff at people
Good girls don't throw stuff at people

Bad boys pick on old people
Good girls don't pick on old people

But girls and boys are still the same
And that's what the teachers say.

Rachel Ingham (9)

GIRLS ON BOYS

Boys are horrible
they're downright mean
they have disgusting habits
they are never clean
their ties are twisted
shirts untucked
laces dangling
their shoes are scuffed
mud on their faces
hair out of place
they think they're better
'But girls are ace!'

Emma Leslie (9)

BOYS AND GIRLS

I hate boys, this is what I think of them.

Boys are made of silliness,
Girls are made of sweetness.
Boys and girls are made for each other,
Unless it is your brother.

Boys are a bit like mice,
Girls are just nice.
Boys and girls can get head lice.

Boys are sometimes a bit rough,
Girls are very tough.
Boys and girls are sometimes gruff.

Boys run away when they are chased,
Maybe us girls should try less haste.
Boys and girls are all part of the human race.

But now it's come to the end of this wonderful grace,
So we all have to go and take our place.

Laura Buckley & Laura Brown (9)

MAKING A FRIEND

Boys collect sticks and stones,
girls collect berries and leaves,
they are ready to make a new snow friend
pile the snow into a heap
then roll a big round ball to make a head.
A carrot for its nose
berries for its eyes,
sticks for its mouth and
autumn leaves for its hair
stones will make lovely buttons for its coat
get a broomstick
get a hat, put them all together
now that is that!

Kirstie Towers (9)

JUST HOW ANNOYING ARE BOYS?

Just how annoying are boys
When you're trying to play with games
And they interrupt with photo frames

Boys are sometimes good
But not always when they should

Just how annoying are boys
When it's pouring down with rain
That's when they become a pain

Boys are sometimes good
But not always when they should

Just how annoying are boys
When you're trying to fill in gaps
And then they're setting up lots of traps

Boys are sometimes good
But not always when they should

I just hope I never get one.

Hayley Burrows (9)

WHAT BOYS PROBABLY THINK ABOUT GIRLS

I don't like girls
None at all,
Not even my sister
Because she hurt me with that big red ball.

I think girls are like
Worms and slugs,
If I could say any better
They look like bugs!

I don't know why
Girls get the attention,
Even at school
I get detention!

Hannah Hartley (9)

GIRLS

Girls?
They're alright I suppose.
They can't play football,
Or cricket, or rugby
But never mind.
Girls?
They're alright I suppose.
Always dreaming of Ronan,
Or Robbie, or 5ive
But never mind.
Girls?
They're alright I suppose.

Thomas Bramley (9)

DIFFERENCES

G iggling girls
I n the latest fashions
R adiant smiles on
L ipsticked lips
S trutting like super models, they are so different from

B oisterous boys
O bsessed with football
Y elling for their
S porting heroes.

Siân O'Keefe (9)

SOME GIRLS

Some girls play football
Some girls ride bikes
But most girls play netball
Because that's what they like.

Girls wear make-up
Girls go shopping
But some play with computers
Without any stopping.

Most girls tell tales
Most girls play with their hair
But some girls giggle
If they don't it's rare.

Nick Morrey (9)

GIRLS, GIRLS, GIRLS

I hate girls because they're crazy
They're silly, stupid and very lazy.
They don't like rugby or football
Because they usually trip and fall.
Dressing up, skipping and dancing
They always talk about who they're fancying.
When they're scared they go red
They might as well go back to bed.
They always seem to chatter and talk
I'd like to prick them with a fork.
They always have such silly toys
I just prefer to play with boys.

Thomas Gornall (9)

BOYS, BOYS, BOYS

Boys tickle girls to get their own way.
Creepy crawlies is a favourite threat.
(What a strange pet)
Ghosts and noise are really boys.
(We know your tricks)
They seem obsessed by cars and all they do.
Boys like fighting, as I look on in horror.
Boasting about their latest bash.
(When it's all really just trash!)
Playing football with their favourite teams.
(In their dreams.)

Natasha Warnock (9)

BOYS

Boys watch the footy,
While the girls go nutty.
Boys think they're witty,
But girls *are* pretty.
While boys are watching the television,
The girls are thinking about fashion.
Boys always munch,
What the girls have made for lunch.
Boys think they're ace,
But they're a waste of space.
Boys are a pest,
So girls *are* the *best*.

Hollie Percival (9)

BOYS ON GIRLS

Girls, girls, girls,
Yuk! Us boys hate girls.
With little pigtails and curls
Plastic beads and pearls
Yuk! Us boys hate girls.

They dress in fancy clothes,
And slop around in high shoes,
These are the species
Us boys want to lose.

They skip in the playground,
Play with cuddly toys,
Why can't they be like us,
Playing on computer games and making lots of noise.

Girls love the boy bands;
Like Boyzone and Westlife.
The boys like Eminem,
Why don't the girls get a life?

The girls meet in the toilets at break,
And each of them tell a funny thing,
Like the jokes that are told on *Friends,*
By the famous Chandler Bing.

Gary Haughan (10)

SLUGS AND SNAILS

Slugs and snails
Puppy dogs' tails

Football, rugby - all sorts of games
That's what they like - and calling girls names

PC, Nintendo, PlayStation 2
Boys are like monkeys messing in a zoo

Liam, Robbie and The Baha Men
Boys all wanna be like Eminem

Britney, Buffy and Destiny's Child
This type of girl drives the boys wild

BMX, skateboard and Gameboys
These are all little boys' toys

With Kevin and Perry on their video
What boy needs any other hero?

Slugs and snails,
Puppy dogs' tails

That's what little boys are made of!

Miggi Nesfield (10)

WHAT GIRLS THINK OF BOYS

Boys can have smelly feet,
but only in a hot heat!
They can be very nice,
and absolutely hate mice!
When it comes down to biting,
they do that when fighting!
Most boys are funny,
and love to eat honey!
Boys like to eat loaves,
when messing up their clothes!
Boys can be messy eaters,
and play around with meters!
If you want to know at all,
they only like to play football!
Boys must make potions,
and hide their emotions!
Loads of blokes
can tell good jokes!
Boys love dying their hair green,
and they hate to be clean!
To sum it up I'd like to add
boys aren't that bad!

Rachael Moses (10)

GIRLS V BOYS

Some people think boys are cool,
But I know the truth.

They stuff their faces with food till they're sick,
They look in the mirror and squeeze their spots,
They spend hours on the loo doing you know what,
They cover their hair with gel till it's greasy,
This is why boys can never be cool,
So . . .
If girls were to battle boys,
I know who would win,
If girls were to battle boys,
I know who would sing,
If girls were to battle boys,
Girls would win,
Girls would win because they're fashionable,
Girls would win because they're fun,
Girls would because they're *best!*

Harriet Doubleday (10)

BOYS

Boys are smelly,
Got brains like jelly.
They think they're good,
But never *never* should
pick on girls
with lovely whirly curls.

Boys do stink,
sometimes wink!
They think it's bliss . . .
. . . to give a girl a kiss!

Boys watch too much telly,
using brains of jelly

Boys play too many games,
using no brains . . .

Girls are best.

Nina Bailey (10)

GIRLS ARE BETTER THAN BOYS

Girls are better than boys because
Girls can run the world,
Girls have more sense of direction,
But most of all girls are better than boys.

Girls are better than boys because
Girls can run forever,
Girls can dance and sing,
But most of all girls are better than boys.

Girls are better than boys because
Girls think deeper thoughts,
Girls are funny,
But most of all girls are better than boys.

Rachel Hayes (10)

I THINK BOYS ARE...

I think boys are . . . *annoying* when they junk up the room,
Annoying when they blame things on you,
They're even *annoying* when you have friends around.

I think boys are . . . *caring* when someone trips or falls,
Caring when you're upset about something that's happened,
They're even *caring* when you're not well.

I think boys are . . . *jealous* when the girl they love has got a boyfriend,
Jealous when girls have been invited somewhere and they haven't,
They're even *jealous* when girls get new, expensive clothes.

I think boys are . . . *fun* if you bribe them,
Fun if they're baby-sitting you and your parents aren't there,
They're even *fun* if you're on holiday.

I think boys are . . . *silly* when they drink alcohol,
Silly when they have their friends round,
They're even *silly* when they go out to a restaurant.

I think boys are . . . *typical* when they're at a footy match,
Typical when their team wins a match,
They're even *typical* when they show off.

I think boys are . . . *unique* in their own way,
Unique in the hobbies they like doing,
They're even *unique* because that's what I think boys are like!

Helen Briggs (10)

WHAT I THINK ABOUT GIRLS!

S ome girls are sweet,
O thers are neat,
M ost are cute,
E very other is minute,
T hey come in different styles,
H eaven is better by miles,
I rresistible they can be,
N ot when they giggle and go . . . he, he,
G orgeous they can be,

A fter they've cooked my tea,
B eautiful and ugly, short and tall,
O nly one will go to the ball,
U sually found chatting,
T own is where they're nattering,

G iving and sharing,
I cing and glaring,
R aging out everywhere,
L ike one little individual pair,
S omething about girls!

Ashley J Williams (10)

SWEETIE

The ship's siren hooted
The captain awaits
The passengers are boarding
Hurry we'll be late
'Nah ya won't sweetie'

He was tall and blonde
Funny and kind
He made me laugh
He danced and sang
'Luv ya sweetie'

Too old for me
I'm far too young
But still I think
With him I'm free
'Come to Oz sweetie'

He played Father Christmas
And sat me on his knee
He kissed me
And hugged me
'Present from Santa sweetie'

We had our photo taken
Which as a gift he gave to me
On the back were words
That showed he cared, and said
'E-mail me sweetie'

I used to hate boys
But the ship had docked
And the tide had turned
Now there is one who I long to return
'Goodbye sweetie.'

Hannah Roberts (10)

HAIR GEL

They say they do it really quick.
Smooth it down, just a flick,
But all they say is not true -
Let me tell you what they do.
In front of the mirror for hours on end,
They drive their mothers round the bend.
Combing and gelling each single hair,
Go into the bathroom if you dare!
Smooth it all down into place -
Then flick it up so it's not in their face.
Oh well, they are boys!

Gemma Hardman (10)

GIRLS ON BOYS

You're mean,
You're selfish,
You're extremely lazy,
You can be brainy or dumb,
Either way you drive girls crazy!

Some of you are OK,
Most of you we hate,
Although there is one man,
Who is none of these,
(Apart from brainy of course!)
He is funny,
And brilliant,
And he is my Dad!

Hannah Hudson (10)

MY LITTLE BROTHER

The boy I know best is my little brother.
Whenever I think of him I shudder.
I think of his hands and the messes they make,
I think of his feet and steps they take.
I think of his brains that would fit in a cup,
And I think of his mouth that never shuts up!
But I love him to bits for he is so clever,
Would you change him for another? No not never,
Would you change him for a cat? No not even that.
Would you change him for a dog? No not even a bird or a frog,
And I still think of his mouth that never shuts up!

Prisca Shallcross (10)

GIRLS ON BOYS

Us girls think about boys,
'I hate the way they laugh at me,'
'I hate the way they stare,
'I hate the way they boss me around,'
And think they know it all.

Us girls think about boys,
'I like the way they play football
And hang around in groups.'
They hold us close when we're upset
But we don't want boys *just yet* . . .

Rachel Chadwick (10)

BAD BOYS, GOOD BOYS

Bad boys are bossy,
Bad boys don't care,
Bad boys go round pulling little girls' hair.

Good boys are helpful,
Good boys are nice,
Good boys don't need asking twice.

Jemma Halliwell (10)

IF I WAS A GIRL

Imagine if I was a girl
Wearing lipstick
Eyeshadow
And pearls
It would be a nightmare
- But -
I am not - how lucky am I
I can wear boxer shorts instead of knickers and bras
Trainers instead of high heels
I am a boy and I am proud of it.

Tom Holmes (10)

BOYS ARE...

Boys are . . .
Boring
No matter what you say they'll always be ignoring
Boys are . . .
Annoying
No matter what you do they're always toying
Boys are . . .
Dopey they always make girls mopey
Boys are . . .
Drippy
They hop around like Skippy
Boys are . . .
Mucky
Bet you none of them are lucky
That's what boys are.

Rachael Bramwell (10)

GIRLS GIRLS GIRLS

Horrible; girls.
Screaming and shouting
a useless thing.
She pulls your hair
and slaps your face.
Her parents say,
'Oh what a waste . . .'
Girls!

She talks so much
your brain goes dead.
Her voice gets right
inside your head.
Louder and louder
until your hearing goes,
telling you all her woes . . .
Girls!

No matter what you say
you feel useless, also shy.
She makes you feel nervous
in every way.
You do your best
you don't know why,
when she will suddenly
start to cry . . .
Girls!

James David Wheatley (11)

BOYS ARE THE BEST

Boys are the best,
Girls are just a pest.
They wouldn't like to run,
They think it's no fun.
They play with boring things,
And say their hands sting,
From just little things.
They eat a lot of sweets and choc,
And end up going to see the doc.
The only games they think are great
Are the games that we boys hate.
At discos they dress like Spice Girls,
And loop around with twists and twirls.
When the music stops the boys leap and bound,
But the boring girls go off in a huff and sit around.
So this is why I think,
All the more,
Boys are the best
And girls are a bore.

James Townsend (11)

GIRLS

Half my class is full of them,
I don't know what to do,
Because they are so different from us,
Perhaps they belong in a zoo!

They are so picky at things,
Like make-up, shopping and shoes.
They are a nightmare at choosing things,
If I go with them I then get the blues.

They love Leonardo and Brad Pitt,
N'Sync, A1 and Westlife,
And they giggle and giggle and giggle,
Would you want one for a wife?

But then they are quite sensible,
Understanding and don't fight,
They can be serious and intelligent,
So perhaps they are alright.

Timothy Diesner (11)

GIRLS ABOUT BOYS!

Boys have very bad habits,
They bite their nails.
They even smell, they're always naughty,
They always chat, the only time they don't
Is when they're watching football on the TV.
When they come to school in the morning
They are always grumpy and bossy.
When we go out at break all they do
Is talk about football, football,
Football and more football.

I really am glad I am not a boy
I really am.

Mairi Campbell

GIRLS ABOUT BOYS

Boys are so smelly after playing sport
(Not that they're not smelly all the time)
Boys are from outer space.
Boys are the most annoying things on earth.
Boys don't have manners.
Boys are weird.
Boys are a waste of time.
Boys are a waste of space.
Boys are lazy.
Boys are couch potatoes.
Boys think they're cool.
When you tell them something
It goes in one ear and out of the other.
The worst thing about boys is their
Personalities!

Mary Jones

BOYS ABOUT GIRLS

Girls are annoying. They are smelly
And have piercings on their bellies.
They are tell tales, bossy and posers
With big noses. Non babe magnets
With no decent clothes.
They ask out the boys every ten minutes.
They're afraid of elephants, snakes,
Tigers, camels, giraffes and gorillas.

Paul O'Hara

GIRLS ABOUT BOYS

Boys lie in bed all day then go downstairs
Get some food, take it back up, put it under the bed
Take it out a couple of months later
Stir it with a mouldy sock, lick it then eat the rest
Then to wash it down they have a cup of mouldy coffee
And when their mums call them for tea
They jump from the banister yelling *'Food I want food'*
When they get to the table whoever's giving them their food
Has to wear protective clothing
But that's nothing compared to what they have to wear
They have to wear goggles, gloves, shower cap and a bucket
under their chin.
Gloves for clean hands (can't be bothered to use cutlery)
Bucket (bibs are too small)
Goggles (to protect their eyes)
Shower cap (so that their hair stays clean)
So if you know what I mean they're just plain *yuk.*

Lauren Buchan

BOYS ABOUT GIRLS

Girls are annoying, girls are stupid,
They ain't got no brains in that tiny little head.
They try to be high, and they think that we're a fly.
Well, that isn't cool, and I ain't no fool.
Girls are soppy, boys are tough.
Girls stay nice, but we can get rough.
Girls think they reign, but they're really insane.
Girls aren't cool, and I think
Boys rule!

Michael Duncan

GIRLS ON BOYS

Boys are so annoying
They always pick their nose
Boys are just disgusting
They stink and smell like toes

Boys are couch potatoes
They moan and groan all day
Boys are just so rowdy
They jump about and scream and shout
Till they get their own way

Boys are so naughty
They lie and cheat every day
Boys are just so rowdy
I wish they would go away!

Laura Brown

GIRLS ON BOYS

Girls rule, boys drool
They can be very sexist
Boys are rubbish at gymnastics (sorry to the boys
That can do gymnastics)

They have no sense of humour and they are slobs
Boys show off a lot about how strong they are
(Which they are not)

Boys fight a lot
They are big babies
Boys put too much gel on their hair and look like a Christmas tree
They *stink* and hate the colour *pink*
They can't sing!
Boys let out wind without letting on!
My wish is that they would grow up!

Alana Grant (11)

BOYS ON GIRLS

Girls are different from boys because
boys don't brush their hair for hours and hours.
They can't play football, boys can.
Girls are good at smudging their make-up.
They make me sick!
I wish girls were nice, funny and kind!
They speak funny and buy clothes
They don't even wear.
They are never helpful, they're very very rude.
I wish girls were nicer looking!

Sam Philip (9)

BOYS ON GIRLS

Girls always moan and shout,
They always go in groups and walk about.
Girls don't do anything exciting or fun,
They just talk and cry.

Girls put on make-up but it just smudges and runs,
They play rubbish music that they go out and buy.
Girls take forever to do their hair,
They play and cuddle their teddy bears.

Girls watch Neighbours and Brookside,
If there's a scary movie on they go behind the sofa and hide.
They can't help annoying us in the playground,
As they are walking around.

I wish girls would disappear off Earth
Or go and live in a compound.

Ross Elliot (11)

BOYS ON GIRLS

Girls spend too much time on their hair
And try to put on make-up but never manage.
They always play with their teddy bears
And show off their hair.

They can't get anything right
And they wear ripped tights.
Girls always seem to crack
And don't eat any decent snacks.

Richard Smith (11)

BOYS ON GIRLS

Girls are different from boys because boys can play football.
They don't sleep until eleven o'clock in the morning.
They never do anything exciting or cool,
And they fancy themselves!
Girls brush their hair for hours, hours, hours, hours,
And one more hour!
Girls spend their life savings on lipstick, earrings, necklaces,
Shampoo and hairspray.

Adam Pollock (10)

BOYS ON GIRLS

Girls spend five hours brushing their hair
Most girls can't play football
Most girls spend all their money on make-up
All girls scream
They always annoy us in the playground
When they make a mistake with their make-up they cry
Girls are rubbish
At
Everything!

Michael Winton (10)

BOYS ON GIRLS

Girls are good at football.
They spend all their money on make-up.
They always jump when they see something scary.
When they see a spider they scream loud.
They moan at everyone.
They brush their hair for hours.
They're scared of spiders, crickets and beetles.

Lawrence Smith (10)

GIRLS ON BOYS

Boys think they're always right
But boys always fight
Boys always talk about football
And if boys play football they always fight.
They always drool over football matches
They're always noisy and burping in front of people
If they were nice the world would
Be a different place altogether and I mean that.

Karyn Pittman (11)

BOYS ON GIRLS

Girls are very bossy,
They can't play football,
Girls argue all the time,
They spend their money on make-up.

Girls never keep secrets,
They slap your wrist,
Girls are scared of everything,
I wish girls didn't exist!

Girls are always telling tales,
Girls watch soaps all the time.
They wear bobbles all the time,
And they scream!

Jamie McDonald (11)

Boys On Girls

Boys are different from girls because
Boys don't play with a piece of rope
And a Barbie doll.
Girls save for ages to just buy make-up
And clothes
And then say 'I don't like this.'
If they see a mouse they jump out of their skin.
I wish girls were nicer looking.
They're manky and rude, they're lazy slobs.
When they're old they look like
Old cracked raisins (some men do too).

Tony Yourston (10)

GIRLS ARE DIFFERENT FROM BOYS BECAUSE . . .

They moan a lot
Some are very pushy
They spend their lives saving for make-up
They go to hairy fairy ballets
They *scream*
They trot like a horse
When they see a mouse all you hear is *help!*
When you say hi all you get is
Get me a glass of cola with ice.
They are not good at team dodgey.
Their throws don't even go 1cm.
They are scared of ants just in case they go up their pants.

James Dickson (10)

GIRLS ON BOYS

Boys are silly
Girls are kinder
Boys say they are better than girls
But they are not
Boys think they are smart at football
They are sometimes bullies.

Kristina Lane (10)

GIRLS ON BOYS

Boys are so annoying
I wish boys would go away
They always kick, punch and hit
Boys annoy me because they think they're always right
Boys think they're good at everything
Boys like dressing up as do teenaged girls
Boys think they are cooler than other people
Boys are the worst people on Earth
Boys are the worst at football
Boys moan when they don't win at football.

Sarah Cowan (11)

GIRLS ON BOYS

Boys are annoying and disgusting
They always fight with each other
Boys like gelling their hair
They never stop talking
Boys like football and like making fun of girls
Boys are really really lazy
They can't stop burping and they always drool over football games.
All boys talk about is football.
They think they are soooo cool but they're not.

Ashleigh Corr (11)

RECIPE TO MAKE A SCHOOLBOY

A handful of jokes
A big bag of footballs,
Gallons of smelly, holey socks,
And a mischievous smile.

A sack full of cunning plans,
A huge crate of crisps and coke
Tons of dirty football kits
And a messy room.

A box full of football trophies
A large book filled with football stickers,
Loads of tracksuits with matching socks,
Mix it all together and what have you got?

Natalie Kerr (11)

ARGUMENT

I wish, I wish, I wish my mum
liked my dad. They keep on arguing
and I get sad. I don't know how it started
it just grew and grew. I've got a little sister
she doesn't mind she looks at them and walks off.
But I'm the one who runs upstairs and cries.
I come downstairs and see my mum sitting on the chair.
I ask her 'Do you like dad?'
'No!'
I ask her why and she explains.
But I am quite over it now.

Jennie Parkin (10)

I Remember When . . .

I remember when I was small
I fell in the mud and lost my ball
I remember when I was small
I stood on the wall and had a big fall

I remember when I was short
I went to Playschool and I was taught
I remember when I was short
I looked at my toe and saw a big wart

I remember when I was little
I ate my food like a rabbit that nibbles
I remember when I was little
I ate all my food with little dribbles.

Rachel Allan (9)

THE PERFECT GIFT

My perfect gift would have to be a rabbit
And it would have to have a bad habit
It would eat a garden pea
Then sit on my settee
And jump up and down on my knee.

The perfect gift would have to be a monkey or
Even a chimpanzee.
It could swing from tree to tree
Then come and cuddle me
Oh, oh, what can it be?
A rabbit, a monkey or a chimpanzee.

Lucy Hutchinson (9)

I REMEMBER WHEN...

I remember the first day at school
It was scary and I did not know what to do.
I remember when I was four years old
I opened my Aunty's door
There was some chocolate in a bowl
I tipped it everywhere and I did not really care.

I remember coming home,
My dad had bought a dog,
I was really happy and excited
And she doesn't smell like a hog.

She is a Springer spaniel called Mandy
And she is so much fun.
Out of all the things that I remember
Mandy is the best one.

Laura Purves (9)

I REMEMBER WAR

I remember war
As bombs hit the floor
Making women weep
And watching thousands of flying sheep.

I remember battle
As bullets killed the cattle
As fire started to flare
You could not see the thousands of dead lying there.

As they soon finish the calamity
There will be lots of dead bodies to see
Animals who live in this place
Will be full of horror and disgrace.

And soon at the end of the fight
There will be a plant in sight
It will be a poppy
To say the world won't carry on being soppy.

Chris Berry (10)

BOYS ABOUT GIRLS

Girls are messy
They paint their nails
Wear high heeled shoes
Ask boys out all the time
They are so bossy

Marc Ramsay (10)

15 THINGS ABOUT BOYS

(1) They don't like to be challenged
(2) They are very afraid of girls
(3) They are extremely crazy
(4) They like to beat each other up
(5) They always make fools of themselves
(6) They are very stupid
(7) I wonder if in the very few brain cells they have,
      if they ever think about anything else except for football,
      football and football.
(8) They are all mummies' boys.
(9) Do boys have any manners at all? Nope.
(10) If a boy had a choice between going out for a family meal
      or staying in watching a football match between two teams
      who they don't even know. They would choose the football.
(11) They don't show their emotions
(12) They are very big-headed. If they answer a simple question
      like 1 + 1 they think they are the best
(13) Boys mature slower than girls, do they actually mature at all?
(14) Don't touch their hair! It takes them all morning to get it right.
(15) In front of their friends they act very hard, but really they are big,
      stupid . . . well all I can really call them are boys.
      Doesn't that say enough?

Helen Price (11)

GIRLS

Girls are mean especially my sister Alia
and one thing I nave noticed is that most
girls smell of something.

Girls have feet that smell like the cheese Jarlsberg
Girls like to be nosy all the time and cry.
Girls don't do anything helpful,
Most girls sleep all day and night.
They are like the living dead but worse
That is what I think, what do you think?

Paul Ian Middleton (10)

BOYS ON GIRLS

Girls are annoying
Their hobbies I think are, jewellery and make-up and
all things stupid.

When they are at school in the playground
All they do is chat when they could be doing something
interesting like kicking a ball about.

Girls are annoying
Their hobbies I think are, jewellery and make-up
and all things stupid.

Most girls are selfish, moany and nasty
when you're in class your teacher always says
'Oh you deserve a star.'

Girls are annoying.
Their hobbies I think are, jewellery and make-up
and all things stupid.

Robert Lindsey (10)

UNTITLED

I know a little girl with blue eyes
And chubby cheeks and long brown hair.
Happy eyes like horse-shoes.
Very cuddly, warm and happy
She cuddles me and kisses me
I am happy.

Michael Harrison (8)

BOYS

Boys, boys look untidy and messy but nice, nice.

Boys, boys always play football or 'stuck in the mud' or 'it'.

Boys, boys - all they do is talk, talk.
I don't know how they do their work, work.

Boys, boys are always picking on everyone
in particular me.

Yasmine Marven (7)

BOYS

Boys think they're cool . . . (Yeah right)
Whilst making girls drool.
But some girls think . . . Boys stink.
Boys think they're so dudey
But they're always so moody.
They think they're smart
Although they always fart.
They think they're ace
At making a base.
Then they grow into men
Oh no!. . . All the same again.

Jennie Walton (9)

BOYS

A   Arrogant
B   Boastful
C   Careless
D   Dorky
E   Eerie
F   Frightful
G   Grumpy
H   Hairy
I   Idiotic
J   Jack-the-lad
K   Killjoys
L   Lazy
M   Mummy's little boys
N   Nasty
O   Odd
P   Pongy
Q   Queasy
R   Rough
S   Silly
T   Thick
U   Ugly
V   Vicious
W   Weird
X   A cross - and that's how they make their mums
Y   Yobs
Z   Zombies

Jenny Harrison (10)

GIRLS ABOUT BOYS

Girls about boys
They are smelly
Annoying, they watch too much TV.

They are grumpy
They are silly on bikes and skateboards.

Anna Kozicki (10)

BOYS ABOUT GIRLS

All girls do is moan, groan and lie on their bums
and don't pay attention, then they get an awful
lot of detention.

If you don't keep you're eyes on them for one second
they put the school on fire and get the hose, when it's done
they do a pose.

Girls don't keep to their diet
I say if they want to, they'd better be really quiet.

Are they just like a Christmas pudding,?
What's wrong with them, I don't know.
This is what I reckon, they're a really old hen.
I don't like them one bit, not even if it was for Jesus.
They're sick, gross, smelly and dirty,
I wish I could poke them with a stick.

Ross Pirie (10)

GIRLS ABOUT BOYS

Boys are always watching TV
when they come home
they smell of school.

Then they go and get
a packet of chips.
They talk about school
and say how boring it is.

I am so glad that I am
not a boy.

Kelsay Renwick (10)

BOYS ON GIRLS

I think girls have no long hair
They are not good at football.
They scream when there is a
fierce dog around.

The girls are scared of mice and rats
They *scream!*
They always *moan* to boys

Girls don't like sisters
Girls don't like boys
Girls always like skipping
Girls are good at moaning
Girls make me scream!
Girls are scared of snakes
Girls are scared of frightening films.

Sulaiman Malik (10)

GIRLS ON BOYS

Boys are more silly than girls
They are not as kind
Boys think they are better than girls
If boys win a game, they brag too much
Some boys think girls can't play football
A lot of boys are messy
Boys tend to fight and bully more
Some boys think too much of themselves!

Stephanie Lawrence (10)

GIRLS ON BOYS

Boys are not polite.
They always fight in the playground.
Boys don't dance properly.
They never miss a football game.
Boys like to wear girls clothes and to wear
Make-up, especially boys in my class.
Boys make me sick!
Boys are *not* good at football.
Boys are very lazy and rude.

Gemma Oliver (10)

THANKS

Was a little urchin
Was living on the street
Was found and taken in
Was made to look so neat

'Long came a kindly soul
Who liked the way I looked
Took me to her home
Where she lived and worked and cooked

For years I was so happy
So bright, so safe, so warm
To have me in your life
For me, it was the norm

But now I'm looking down
From a place that's called 'Cat Heaven'
I thank you for the nice times
Until I was eleven

Remember all the mischief
Was never told to stop it
I know you won't forget me, Mum,
My name was little Poppet.

James Galloway